Setting Up Your AQUARIUM

by Mary Ginder

Scientific Consultant:
Dorene Bolze, aquarist and international consultant
on aquatic environment studies.

© 2004 Dalmatian Press, LLC
All rights reserved. Printed in the U.S.A.

Fish Photos©William Zarnick, Animal Graphics
Designer *Dan Waters*
ISBN: 1-40371-202-6

13795 Setting Up and Caring For Your Aquarium
04 05 06 07 WWP 10 9 8 7 6 5 4 3 2 1

Introduction

What a wonderful hobby you've chosen! With very little effort, you will thoroughly enjoy your aquarium and tropical fish. An aquarium is a handsome addition to any room, plus it offers fascinating, relaxing entertainment to children and adults.

I was captivated by the small aquarium my mother set up of basic freshwater community fish when I was no more than four years old. It was a window into the world around me and for me formed the foundation of my interest in biology.

Most of us do not think about where aquarium fish or plants come from. Yet, this is critical, since many barrier reefs, freshwater rivers in the tropics (such as the Amazon), and oceans are being harmed by over-collection. So, becoming a responsible, knowledgeable aquarist is important.

Most freshwater aquarium fish are not caught in the wild but are bred in hatchery ponds. The most important thing an aquarium owner can do to protect the aquatic world is to select fish from captivity. After you start your freshwater aquarium with the common aquarium fish and you want to get more specialized, please do the research on the fish you are interested in to see where they come from. You can even become part of a network of breeders of species of fish.

The references in the back of this book will get you started in finding out about which tropical fish are safe to enjoy and which to avoid—so that your love of fish and having an aquarium also protects your favorite fish in the wild rivers, reefs, and oceans.

You will find this book to be helpful and informative in setting up your freshwater aquarium. It also offers invaluable tips for long-term success and enjoyment—for you *and* for the animals and plants in your care.

Have fun—relax—and enjoy!

Dorene Bolze
Executive Director
Harpeth River Watershed Association
Franklin, Tennessee
http:\\www.harpethriver.org
Working Together to Protect and Restore the Harpeth River

Contents

Your First Aquarium, Step-by-Step

Before you start buying fish and aquarium equipment, take the time to read this book and learn how to choose, set up, and care for your new pets and their aquatic home. You'll find additional resources, including helpful websites, listed at the back of the book. A little preparation will make it easy to keep your fish healthy—and happy!

1. **PLAN:** Decide on the size and location of your aquarium (don't forget to measure!), and use the shopping list on page 6 to make a list of the necessary equipment and supplies (light, filter, etc.). Learn more in Chapter 1.

2. **PURCHASE:** Now it's time to bring home the aquarium and equipment, but **on this first shopping trip DO NOT buy fish!** You need to set up the aquarium and wait at least 2–3 days before adding fish.

3. **INSTALL:** Set up the aquarium following the manufacturer's directions and our tips in Chapters 2 and 3. During this stage, you will fill the tank with water; make the water suitable for fish; and install the heater, light, and other equipment.

4. **ADD FISH:** Read Chapter 4 to learn how to choose your fish, acclimate them to their new home, and take care of them. **Aquarium experts recommend that you initially buy only half the fish (groups of 3 or 4 at the most) that the tank will hold. These starter fish will transform your sparkling new tank into a "mature" tank with the friendly bacteria necessary to process ammonia and other wastes.**

5. **SCHEDULE:** Create and follow a regular schedule for feeding the fish (be careful not to feed them too much or too often) and for maintaining the tank. Use our handy checklist on page 53.

FIRST THINGS FIRST
Planning Your Aquarium

Location

Where will you put your new aquarium? Obviously you want to set it up in a room where you can enjoy watching the fish, but there are a few additional factors to consider:

✔ Place the tank in a part of the room where you can easily control the temperature and lighting. Avoid direct sunlight, vents, or places near frequently opened (drafty) doors.

✔ The fish will get used to being around people if you put the tank in a room that's frequently used. Avoid high traffic areas, however, or places where the tank may be bumped.

✔ Make sure you have convenient access to all sides of the tank for cleaning and maintenance.

✔ Check to see that there is a nearby electrical outlet for the filter and other equipment.

✔ Is there a faucet reasonably close by? You'll be carrying buckets of water back and forth.

✔ Remember, tanks filled with water—even small tanks—are very heavy! Large tanks (100+ gallons) may need to be placed near weight-bearing walls.

Shopping List

Buy these items first:

- ❏ **Aquarium**
- ❏ **Aquarium stand**
- ❏ **Aquarium cover including fluorescent light**
- ❏ **Filtration system**
- ❏ **Air pump** (optional)
- ❏ **Heater** (automatic is best)
- ❏ **Thermometer**
- ❏ **Water conditioner**
- ❏ **Gravel**
- ❏ **Fish net**
- ❏ **Decorative background** (optional)
- ❏ **Plants and decorations**
- ❏ **Gravel vacuum**
- ❏ **Algae scrubber**
- ❏ **Test kits (pH, ammonia, nitrites)**
- ❏ **Two 5-gallon plastic buckets**

Hey, what about the fish?

No, we didn't forget the fish! That's the whole reason
you want the aquarium, right? But you won't be ready
to buy the fish until you have the aquarium set up with
the temperature and water quality under control.
So wait at least 24–48 hours to bring your new fish home.
In chapter 3, we'll explain why this pause in the process
is so important.

On your second shopping trip, buy:

- ❏ **Fish** (about 1/2 the tank will hold)
- ❏ **Fish food**

Aquarium Kits

Aquarium kits make it easy for the beginning fishkeeper to get what they need, or at least most of it, in one package. Most of these starter kits include the fish tank as well as a heater and a filtration system. Other items may also be included, so check the outside of the box carefully and compare it to your shopping list to see what you need to buy separately.

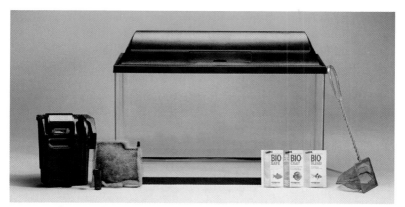

Starter kits, which include the heater and filter, are available with tanks in several different sizes.

Choosing an Aquarium

SIZE: A common mistake is thinking that a small tank (10-gallons or less) will be easier for beginners to manage. Not so! A 20- to 30-gallon tank is actually a great size for most beginners. You'll find it easier to maintain a stable, healthy environment in a medium-sized tank, which means you'll lose fewer fish. The fish will have more room to get away from each other, too, which reduces aggression problems. Best of all, more room in the tank means you'll have more fish to watch!

However, if space is limited, "mini-tanks" come in many shapes and sizes. Select one that includes a light and heater. Remember, however, that a small tank can comfortably hold only a few fish (regardless of how many are pictured on the box it comes in). Resist the urge to relive your childhood days by getting a fish bowl. They're hard to keep clean and even a single fish will find them confining. It's no fun to have goldfish for the kids if you're constantly having goldfish funerals.

SHAPE: Aquarium tanks come in many different shapes, everything from the traditional rectangular ones to round ones, bow-fronts, or tall narrow columns. What kind would fit best in the space you have available? We recommend wider tanks (rather than tall narrow ones) since they have more surface area and make it easier for oxygen to enter the water at its surface. Fish prefer to swim side-to-side, too! (Plus, taller tanks can be harder to clean.)

GLASS vs. ACRYLIC: Either is a good choice. Glass tanks are heavier and somewhat easier to break. On the other hand, acrylic tanks scratch more easily than glass tanks, and you will need to remember that when cleaning them. However, most acrylic scratches can be fixed so this isn't much of a disadvantage.

Aquarium Stands

As tempting as it might be to save some money and place the aquarium on a table you already have, the safest strategy is to purchase a stand that's designed specifically to provide a steady, level surface for your aquarium. The larger the aquarium, the more important it is to have a well-made stand to support it. Just consider this—a 50-gallon tank filled with water weighs more than 400 pounds!

Choose a stand that's sturdy enough to hold a tank of your size and that fits well with your décor. Some offer storage compartments that keep fish food and other supplies conveniently close by yet out of sight.

SAFETY WARNING
Never place an aquarium on top of an entertainment center, or above or below electrical appliances.

Lights and Covers

Lighting makes your aquarium look more beautiful and allows you to see the fish. (The light becomes even more important if you add live plants to your aquarium, though we don't recommend working with live plants until you are more experienced.) Also, the light provides your fish with the needed UV light that the glass of the tank filters out.

Most aquarium owners buy a fluorescent tube lighting system that is part of a "full-hood" plastic cover. This covers the entire top and provides a hinged lid so you can easily feed the fish. The cover keeps adventurous fish from jumping out and adventurous kids and pets from reaching in. For best fit, buy a cover made by the same manufacturer as your aquarium tank.

For 55-gallon and larger aquariums, you will want a twin-tube fluorescent light rather than just a single bulb. When it comes time to change bulbs, choose fluorescent bulbs designed specifically for aquarium use.

Filtration Systems

You won't be surprised to learn that fish need clean, clear water. That's why aquariums require filtration systems. In natural habitats, moving water dilutes wastes and pollution, but in an aquarium these tasks must be taken care of in other ways. Filters remove wastes and oxygenate (add oxygen to) the water. Without proper filtering, your fish will suffocate and die—it's that simple.

An aquarium needs three kinds of filtration to keep fish healthy (trust us, you need to know this):

1. **MECHANICAL FILTRATION:** The filter traps solid waste particles including fish wastes and uneaten food.

2. **BIOLOGICAL FILTRATION:** Fish excrete (put out) ammonia as a waste product. If too much ammonia builds up in the water, the fish will die. Biological filtration uses "friendly bacteria" to remove ammonia and other organic wastes.

3. **CHEMICAL FILTRATION:** Filters contain activated carbon or other material which bonds with chlorine, ammonia, phosphate, dyes, etc., that have dissolved into the water.

There are several kinds of filters available. **Whichever type you buy, check the package carefully to make sure that it is the right choice for the size of your aquarium.** In some cases, it will take more than one kind of filter to provide all three types of filtration.

POWER FILTERS: The easiest way to provide mechanical, biological and chemical filtration with just one unit is to purchase a power filter. These usually hang on the back of your tank. Water is siphoned out of the tank, pumped through the filter material and then returned to the tank. The cartridge in the power filter soaks up the wastes and needs to be replaced periodically. Power filters are a good option for tanks up to about 50-gallons in size.

CANISTER FILTERS: Canister filters are more powerful and so make the best choice for larger tanks. Most models sit on the floor beneath the aquarium but some hang on the back like power filters. They provide stronger mechanical filtration than

Affordable power filters are great choices for beginners.

do power filters, but provide limited biological filtration and need to be cleaned frequently for most effective operation.

UNDERGRAVEL FILTERS: As the name suggests, undergravel filters are installed at the bottom of the tank and covered with gravel. The gravel traps the solid waste particles as water is pulled down through it by the filter. Although they require fairly little maintenance, proper set-up can be complicated and we recommend that beginners start out with power filters instead.

If you decide to use an undergravel filter, be aware of two things: First, the undergravel filter alone does not provide chemical filtration so you will need to use a special carbon cartridge (if the filter model supports it) or add a power filter. Second, because the gravel at the bottom of the tank is essential to the filtration process, you will need to use your gravel vacuum often and regularly to keep it clean.

Air Pumps

Filters help circulate water, so an air pump isn't absolutely necessary for all aquarium owners. But an air pump will increase water circulation, increase the amount of oxygen taken in at the surface, and help carbon dioxide and other waste products escape. They can also be used to power airstones, bubblers, and some kinds of decorations, so you may want to purchase an air pump right at the start.

Check the air pump package to see whether you need to purchase air hoses or valves separately.

Air pumps help increase water circulation and oxygenation.

AIRSTONES: These porous artificial stones are used to break air bubbles produced by the pump into tinier bubbles. They help oxygenate the water (and let's be honest, the bubbles are fun to watch).

Heaters and Thermometers

Most types of tropical fish need the water temperature to be a stable 75–79°F (23.8–26.1°C). Goldfish are an exception—they prefer cooler temperatures, 62–65°F (16.6–18.3°C), which is why they can be kept in tanks without heaters.

A submersible heater is necessary for most tropical fish tanks, though gold-fish tanks may not need them.

To maintain a stable temperature in the tank, regardless of the temperature in the room, you'll need a heater. In most cases, it will be a combination heater-thermostat which is submerged in the water at the back or side of the tank.

How big does the heater need to be? Generally, you want 5 watts of heater per gallon, so a 30-gallon tank would require a 150-watt heater. It should say right on the heater package what size tanks it will handle. This is usually given as a range: "10–30" indicates the heater will heat tanks from 10 to 30 gallons.

Larger tanks (55-gallon and up) benefit from having two lower-wattage heaters instead of a single high-wattage heater. Having two helps maintain a constant temperature throughout the tank and gives you a backup in case one stops working.

You will also need a thermometer to verify that the temperature stays in the desired range. Buy one that floats inside the tank or a digital one that sticks on the outside of the tank —both types are pretty accurate.

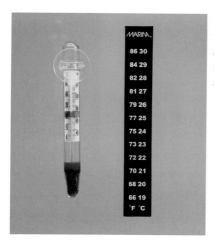

You can choose a floating thermometer or a digital strip version that adheres to the outside of the tank.

Water Conditioner and Test Kits

Would you believe that the water that comes out of the faucet in your home can be harmful to fish, even if it's very clean and perfectly safe for you to drink? It's true. Here's what you need to buy, and why, to prepare water for use in the tank, and to check water quality:

WATER CONDITIONER (also known as DECHLORINATOR): The chlorine that's added to tap water kills germs, but even tiny amounts of chlorine in an aquarium can kill the fish. After filling your tank, you need to use a "dechlorinating" water

conditioner to neutralize the chlorine. There are several products on the market now which not only dechlorinate, but promote the growth of the friendly bacteria you need to handle the wastes that will

Special water conditioning products remove chlorine and chloramines, provide fish with a protective slime coating for their fins, and jumpstart the friendly bacteria that help process wastes in the tank.

build up in the tank. Some of these remedies even provide a
coating for the fish which helps protect their fins and scales.

NOTE: There may be chloramine or other additives which need
to be neutralized in the tapwater in your area. Ask your local
pet store if additional measures are needed to prepare tap
water for aquarium use.

pH TEST KIT: pH is a measure of whether a substance is acidic
(pH less than 7) or alkalinic (pH greater than 7). A value of 7.0
on the pH scale is considered neutral. The pH of the water in a
fish tank will vary depending on the types of materials which
have been dissolved into the water. For that reason you should
check the pH level periodically. Most tropical fish do well in
water that tests
in the 6–8 pH
range (in other
words, as close to
neutral, 7.0, as
possible).

**AMMONIA AND
NITRITE TEST KITS:**
Ammonia,
nitrites, and
nitrates all build
up in the water
of your aquarium
from fish
excretion and
other natural
processes.
In natural
environments,

*Test kits for pH level and ammonia are
not only quick and easy to use, but
essential to keeping the water in your
aquarium safe for fish.*

these would be diluted by large amounts of moving water, but in the smaller enclosed world of the aquarium they need to be removed by filtration and water changes. Ammonia and nitrite test kits are key to monitoring water quality.

WATER HARDNESS TEST KIT: The "hardness" of water indicates the amount of calcium and magnesium it contains. You only have to worry about this if your water is extremely hard or extremely soft. You can ask a local aquarium expert about this or buy a simple test kit to check it yourself.

Other Equipment

Once your aquarium is set up and stocked, you will quickly get into a routine for doing the "housework" that keeps the tank in good working order. Here are the supplies you'll need:

GRAVEL VACUUM: You simply can't get along without one of these handy tools. In addition to sucking up waste particles from the gravel, the gravel can also be used to siphon water from the tank during partial water changes. (You'll learn more about this in Chapter 5.)

A gravel vacuum cleaner makes cleaning more efficient and keeps your tank healthy.

ALGAE SCRAPER OR SCRUBBER PADS: These are special scrapers or pads used for cleaning algae growth from the inside walls of the aquarium. **DO NOT substitute regular household sponges as they have been treated with chemicals which will be harmful to the fish.** If your tank is acrylic, be careful to use only algae scrubber pads that are suitable for acrylic, otherwise you may scratch the walls. The newer magnetic ones allow you to scrub the inside glass without even putting your hands in the tank!

PLASTIC BUCKET: You'll need two clean plastic buckets, about 5-gallons in size, for water changes. Buy new buckets specifically for this purpose so that they will contain no traces of soap or cleaning chemicals. Use these for aquarium purposes ONLY—label them to make sure everyone in the house honors this.

FISH NET: Every fishkeeper needs at least one long-handled fish net for scooping up fish. You may find as you gain experience that it's helpful to have some in different sizes.

Gravel

You need enough gravel to form a layer 1–2 inches deep at the bottom of the aquarium. The gravel (also known as "substrate") is more than just decorative, it will become home to helpful bacteria that process wastes and will also provide footing for plants and decorative items added to the tank. Gravel comes in many different grain sizes. A small to medium-size grain will be less likely to pack down than fine-grained sand. This is especially important if your tank has an undergravel filter. However, too large a size grain will make it easier for food to sink into the gravel where the fish can't reach it.

Gravel comes in many different grain sizes and colors.
You can also add aquarium-safe stones and glass beads.

Gravel comes in many different colors and what you choose is largely a matter of personal preference. Some people think that fish are more visible against a dark background.

Plants and Decorations

Decorating your aquarium is a lot like decorating your home —it's mostly a matter of personal style, but there are some practical considerations, too.

PLANTS: The main reason to place plants in aquariums is to provide cover (hiding places) for the fish. The other reason is that they look good! While some people insist on live plants, we encourage those new to the hobby to stick with the plastic ones. Many expert aquarists prefer plastic plants, which require no maintenance except for an occasional cleaning.

Choose from realistic-looking artificial plants or try some of the "glow in the dark" or other fun varieties.

BACKGROUND: Many people like to add a decorative background to complete the look of their aquarium (and to hide the cords and other equipment behind the tank). These are usually two-dimensional scenes that tape onto the back of the tank, but submersible three-dimensional ones are also available.

ROCKS AND WOOD: As with plants, this is another time when the "real thing" may not be the best choice for your aquarium. Instead of collecting your own rocks, and possibly introducing chemicals to your aquarium that will alter the water chemistry and harm your fish, buy the aquarium-safe variety sold at your local fish store or pet shop. Artificial rocks may also be available there. Likewise, real wood pieces would require time-consuming preparation to make them safe for use in your aquarium, so stick with the artificial driftwood pieces at the pet shop.

ARTIFICIAL ITEMS: Need a few mermaids to liven up the scene? How about one of those sunken ships and a deep sea diver? No matter where you buy your aquarium, chances are they'll have an interesting selection of decorative items.

Decorations for fish tanks range from subtle and elegant to funky and wild. It's not hard to find something you like! The fish aren't terribly fussy about what the decorations look like—they just like ones that provide lots of hiding places.

READY, SET, GO
Setting Up the Equipment

Now you'll enter the most time-consuming stage of getting your first aquarium up and running—putting all the pieces together. But it is well worth the time it takes to do it right and that means, you guessed it, pausing to **READ THE DIRECTIONS** that come with the tank and other components. Do that now!

Get Ready...

1. **Wash out the tank** with clean water and either a paper towel or a soft new sponge. (Don't use an old sponge as it may have traces of soap or cleaning products on it.)

2. It is unlikely that a new tank will have any leaks, but if you have purchased a secondhand tank, it's a good idea to **check for leaks**. Find a level place to set the tank and fill it with water. Make sure the area around the tank is dry, so if you find water later on you'll know it's from a tank leak. Let the tank sit for several hours. To avoid a mess, you may want to do this outside.

3. Using a strainer, **rinse the gravel** thoroughly with clean water. Wash your decorative items and plastic plants, too.

Get Set...

1. **Set up your aquarium stand.** It must be stable and level. If necessary, add some narrow wood pieces beneath it to bring it into level. Remember to leave room behind it and

on the sides so that you can install equipment and do your
routine maintenance on the tank. Make sure too that you
have an electrical outlet close by for the heater, filter, and
light. You won't be able to move the aquarium once it's filled
with water, so now's the time to make sure that the location
you've chosen is going to work well.

2. **Put the aquarium on the stand.** Is it steady and secure?
   Does it fit properly without hanging over the edges?

3. Tape the **decorative background** to the back of
   the tank.

4. If you purchased an **undergravel filter,** install it now.
   DO NOT PLUG IT IN YET.

5. **Add the gravel.** It should be about 2 inches deep.
   Making it a little deeper in the back helps hold your
   decorations in place and lets waste particles float
   down toward the front where they're easier to reach
   with the gravel vacuum.

6. If you're using a **power filter,** follow the manufacturer's
   instructions to install it. These often require that water be
   added to "prime" the filter. DO NOT PLUG IT IN YET.

7. If you purchased an **air pump,** install it now.
   DO NOT PLUG IT IN YET.

8. **Install your heater** now at the back of the tank, following the
   manufacturer's instructions. DO NOT PLUG IT IN YET.

9. **Add the heavier decorations** now. Lighter ones, including plants, are best added after the tank is filled with water. If you purchased **airstones,** you can add these now, too.

10. Now you're ready to **fill the tank.** The water should be as close to room temperature as possible. Before you start, put a small plate or dish on top of the gravel. Then pour the water onto the plate and this will keep it from shifting the gravel and decorations.

11. **Add plants and any other decorations** now.

12. **Add water conditioner (dechlorinator)** to the tank, following the directions on the package.

13. Now **use your pH test kit.** If the pH is in the normal range, usually between 6–8, great. If not, see the box titled "Fixing pH and Ammonia Problems" in this chapter.

Go!

1. **Plug in the heater.** SAFETY WARNING: Never plug in a heater unless it is properly submerged in the tank. If you need to remove the heater, unplug it and allow it to cool in the water before taking it out of the tank.

2. **Install your thermometer** in a part of the tank where it won't block your view of the fish. Most types either stick on the side of the tank or float in the water.

3. Wait at least 15 minutes after plugging in the heater and then **check the temperature** in the tank. Adjust the heater as needed. It may take up to 24 hours to gradually get the temperature stabilized where you want it to be.

4. **Plug in the filter and air pump.**

5. Put the cover on the tank and **plug in the light.**

6. **Now comes the hardest step of all... you have to WAIT!** The aquarium needs to run 2–3 days before you add fish. (For the really impatient fishkeeper, 24 hours is the

absolute minimum you MUST allow before adding the fish.) This time ensures that your aquarium has a stable temperature, appropriate pH level, and gives the bacteria needed to handle ammonia and other waste products time to start getting established.

7. **After the waiting period in step #6 is done, check the pH level and temperature in the tank.** If they're in the normal range for your chosen fish, go on to the next step. If not:

FIXING pH AND AMMONIA PROBLEMS
For nearly any kind of water quality problem—pH too high or low, ammonia or nitrites too high, etc.—there are a variety of products on the market to help you resolve it. Be careful when you add these chemicals to the aquarium, however. Make changes very gradually. It's better to add too little and adjust levels very slowly than to make dramatic changes that will worsen the stress on your fish.

You can also buy a test kit to check for nitrates, the end result of the ammonia-nitrite-nitrate breakdown process, also known as the "nitrogen cycle," but the only solution for too many nitrates is to do a partial water change (and do them regularly).

8. **Add your "starter fish."** This should be a small batch (3 to 4 fish) of hardy (and inexpensive) fish, not the entire community that you intend to have when the tank is up and running. These first few fish continue the process of building up the right bacteria and establishing proper water chemistry. Use your ammonia and nitrite test kits to see that the process is proceeding as it should (see Chapter 3). When this first "cycle" is complete, you can add more fish.

9. Set up a plan for **daily feeding and regular maintenance.** See Chapter 4 for all the details.

10. **Congratulate yourself** on a job well done. Pull up a chair and get to know your new pets!

CLEAN WATER
Managing Water Quality

WATER QUALITY

In the great outdoors, water is naturally filtered, constantly moving and being diluted by the addition of rainwater and water from adjoining streams and rivers. In the very small environment of your aquarium, these processes are managed through heating, filtration, and human intervention.

Unlike dogs and cats, fish don't have to be housebroken, but they still produce waste products which need to be taken care of. The good news is that you will have a million tiny helpers in this process—colonies of friendly bacteria that will quickly grow in the aquarium to help dispose of wastes. (And the fish will never wake you up in the middle of the night wanting to go outside!)

Here's how it works...

Cycling Your Tank

Fish use food to make energy, just like we do, and they use the oxygen they breathe in from the water to help with this process. The main waste products that result are **carbon dioxide** and **ammonia**. The carbon dioxide is taken care of by aeration (air exchange) at the surface of the tank. It takes a little more effort to take care of the ammonia and related wastes.

Even a low level of ammonia in the tank is toxic and will kill your fish. This is where a set of biological and chemical processes, known as the nitrogen cycle, come into play. Bacteria soon arrive on the scene that break the ammonia

23

CLOUDY WATER?
Don't be surprised if the water gets cloudy during
the first cycle. This is completely normal and you
do not need to do anything about it. The cloudiness should
go away on its own within a few days. If it
doesn't, there are commercial products available
to help clear things up.

down into nitrite. Unfortunately, nitrite is still toxic for your fish. But the good news is that yet another type of bacteria converts the **nitrite** into **nitrate**. The nitrate is much less dangerous for the fish and will be handled by routine partial water changes. (Sorry, this is a job you have to do—the bacteria can't carry the buckets. More details to come.)

STARTER FISH: In the previous chapter, we told you to begin with only a few "starter fish" after you set up the tank. Don't start out with the most finicky (or most expensive!) fish that you want to keep, just in case the worst happens. Start small! As soon as they are added into the tank, these fish will start excreting ammonia. Test the ammonia level every 1 to 3 days and you will see that it continues to go up for the first week or two, then falls back down to zero. That means that the bacteria are doing their job to convert the ammonia into nitrite.

But remember that nitrite is also toxic for the fish. So test the nitrite level every 2 to 3 days during this stage, too. Like the ammonia level, it will climb for about 7–14 days and then fall back to zero. It will reach zero a few days after the ammonia level does.

When both the ammonia and nitrite levels have gone back to zero, they have been converted into the safer nitrates and the cycle is complete. Now you can add more fish! But not too many—an easy beginner mistake is overloading the tank with too many fish. That makes it impossible to keep up with the ammonia and nitrite wastes and fish will die. (Check out Chapter 4 before you head back to the fish store.)

NEW TANK SYNDROME

"New Tank Syndrome" is what happens when new aquarium owners get too enthusiastic. They fill the aquarium to the brim with fish before it's had time to let the helpful bacteria colonize. Ammonia and nitrite levels rise very rapidly and most or all of the fish die. This can happen within a matter of days. We've said it before—it's worth taking the time to do it right! Make sure you let the tank cycle properly before adding more fish.

Testing Water Conditions

Even after you've successfully cycled your aquarium, you will want to set up a schedule for periodically checking various aspects of water quality. This will also be the first thing to do in case your fish appear to be getting sick.

These test kits may sound intimidating but they are actually quite easy to use. Just follow the directions! Here are the most commonly checked levels:

AMMONIA AND NITRITE: Testing for ammonia and nitrite is critically important when cycling the new aquarium. Once your tank is well established, however, you will only need to check these if the fish look like they are suffering or getting sick. Sticking to your schedule for partial water changes, at least every 2 weeks, will help keep wastes from building up. If you still find that ammonia or nitrite levels are higher than they should be, your tank may be overstocked and wastes may be building up faster than the filtration system can handle. You can also test for nitrates—if the level is high, you may not be doing your partial water changes often enough.

pH: The pH scale goes from 0–14, where 7.0 is neutral. Values less than 7.0 are acidic, and values over 7.0 are alkalinic. While some types of fish have different pH requirements, most will do fine in a tank where the pH is near neutral, between 6 and 8. Small variations within this range are usually not a problem. However, if pH is too high or low, your fish will suffer. Check your pH every 1–2 weeks.

Special chemicals are available to help adjust pH levels and can be purchased in fish stores and pet shops. These should be used very carefully since over-correcting the problem just makes things more stressful for the fish. Follow the manufacturer's instructions carefully.

WATER HARDNESS: You probably won't need to worry about testing for water hardness, a measure of how much magnesium, calcium and other minerals are dissolved into the water. However, if you know that water in your area is considered to be very hard or very soft, buy a carbonate hardness kit at your fish store.

Partial Water Changes

The filtration system and all those helpful bacteria we've talked about do a lot of work in removing wastes from the aquarium, but they can't do a perfect job of it. That's why it's necessary to do a "partial water change," removing and replacing about 20% of the water in the tank, once a month. (Replacing 10–15% of the water each week is even better, if you have the time to do it. But replacing more water less often than once a month is NOT the way to go—the shock of such dramatic changes is harmful for the fish.)

Water changes help dilute nitrates and replace beneficial trace elements which are lost to filtration. The end result: fish are healthier and live longer.

Since other routine maintenance can be conveniently done during the water change process, we'll cover the details on changing the water in Chapter 5.

DOES THIS COUNT?
You may occasionally want to "top off the tank" by adding more (dechlorinated) water to replace what evaporates from the aquarium. **This does not count as a partial water change!** Evaporation does not remove the waste products, it only removes the water.

FISH FACTS
How to Select and Care for Tropical Fish

You're in the fish store standing in front of all those tanks filled with fish. So many beautiful fish to choose from, how will you decide which ones to bring home? Well, picking at random based on how pretty they are is not the best way. A little careful planning will help ensure that the fish you choose are well suited for your tank and that they will be compatible with each other.

How Many Fish Can I Have?

Glad you asked that question first! Beginners often run into trouble because they buy too many fish—the tank becomes overcrowded, wastes build up too fast, and fish die. So avoid overcrowding by using this basic guideline:

ONE INCH (2.5CM) OF FISH PER GALLON OF WATER

For example, if you have a 55-gallon tank, you can have up to 55 fish assuming they are 1 inch long or shorter. (Tails don't count in the length measurement.) If you have a 10-gallon tank, you could have up to 10 fish that are 1-inch long or shorter.

This formula works for fish that are up to about 3 inches in length. So going back to our 55-gallon tank, instead of 55 fish that are 1 inch long, you could have 27 fish that are each about 2 inches long.

When you start looking at fish that are more than 3 inches in length, things get trickier because the fish aren't just longer, they're also wider and taller. While a 1-inch fish needs 1 gallon of water, a 4-inch fish needs 5 gallons of water—which means that your 55-gallon tank would only hold 11 of these larger fish. Unless you have a very large tank and a good understanding of how to care for these larger fish, we recommend sticking with the smaller ones when starting out. You wouldn't try to raise Labrador retrievers if you lived in a tiny studio apartment, would you? Likewise, it's unfair to the fish to put them in tanks that are too small for them.

How Do I Choose?

There are some things you'll want to know about each species of fish that you consider for your aquarium. Will they do well in the type of tank environment that you have? Will they get along with the other types of fish you have or plan to buy? Most fish stores provide labels on the tanks to tell you more about each type of fish and its basic requirements. Here's what you'll want to find out:

❑ **Will this fish do well in the pH level and temperature I've established in my tank?** If its requirements are too different, it's not a good choice. For example, mixing tropical fish and goldfish in the same tank usually doesn't work well because their temperature needs are too different.

❑ **Is it fussy or tolerant regarding variations in ammonia and nitrite levels?** Make your life easier with this first tank and choose species like mollies and guppies that aren't going to die from small variations in water conditions. Give yourself some time to be comfortable with managing the tank before you purchase fish with more complicated requirements.

❑ **How big will it get?** Just because it's a tiny little thing in the store tank doesn't mean it's going to stay that way. Most of the fish you see in stores are still in their baby days. Fish grow—and some types never seem to stop growing! It can also be problematic if one type of fish in the tank grows a lot faster than the others do—big fish tend to eat little fish!

❑ **How long does it usually live?**

❑ **What kind of food does it like?**

❑ **Does it feed mostly during the day or at night?** Balance night-feeding (nocturnal) species with ones that come out to feed during the daytime, otherwise the tank will be very boring to watch.

❑ **Does it spend most of its time at the top of the tank, middle of the tank, or bottom of the tank?** Getting a good mix of fish that prefer the different levels in the tank reduces compatibility problems (they all have their own space!) and means there will be more activity for you to watch.

❑ **Does it need a lot of hiding places?** If it does, you may need to add some plants or other decorative items to allow it more cover.

❑ **Does it need to be with other fish of the same type to be happy?** This is called "schooling behavior." Fish that like to school will be much happier (and less likely to bother your other fish) if they have at least 3–4 fish of the same species to keep them company.

❑ **Is it territorial?** Will it stake a claim to a particular portion of the tank? Be careful to introduce only a very few (or even no) fish that are territorial or they will fight to protect their favorite spots.

FISH FACTS

DO THEY WORK WELL AND PLAY WELL WITH OTHERS?
The smaller the tank, the more difficult it is to manage compatibility problems—the fish just don't have enough room to get away from each other.

❏ **it get along with my other fish?** Find out whether the species tends to be especially aggressive. Are they "fin-nippers" who nibble at the fins of other fish? In that case, don't combine them with fish who have long fins. Having lots of hiding places is very helpful for reducing the fish-eating-other-fish problem.

❏ **Any other special requirements?** For example, do you need to have a certain number of female fish to each male in this species?

Selecting Healthy Fish

No one wants to waste money buying sick fish or, worse yet, to bring home sick fish that will infect others in your aquarium.

HEALTHY FISH: Generally speaking, healthy fish swim easily and breathe easily. Their scales are free of sores. Their fins are intact, without ragged edges or rips, and are not held tight against their bodies. Eyes and lips are clean and without obvious infection. Their bellies may be rounded but are not swollen.

SICK FISH: Don't buy a fish that is sluggish, breathes raggedly, shows sores or ulcers, or has white spots sprinkled across the skin. Tiny white spots can be a sign of "ich," an infection that spreads very easily to other fish. You should also be cautious if the fish appears to be off-color compared to others of the same

WELCOME TO THE "COMMUNITY TANK"

In the fish store, "community fish" or "community tank" labels indicate that the fish species will do well in a tank with other varieties. They will not be very aggressive and will stay relatively small.

You will also hear or read about the "species tank," which is a tank containing primarily a single species of fish. This is the approach if you want to raise more aggressive fish that don't get along well with others.

species and gender or if it is resting either at the top of the tank or the bottom (although in some species that resting behavior is normal). Of course, if there are dead fish in the store's tank, buy your fish somewhere else!

Good Choices for Beginners

When you're just starting out, look for species of fish that are hardy (not likely to die from minor variations in water conditions) and that get along well with others. As we mentioned earlier, overcrowding the tank with too many fish will cause wastes to build up too fast and may also worsen compatibility problems between the fish (see "How Many Fish Will Fit?" earlier in this chapter).

GOLDFISH AND FRIENDS: For a lot of people, especially kids, an aquarium just wouldn't feel right without some goldfish in it. The "common goldfish" is a nice choice for your aquarium, but remember that it prefers cooler temperatures than many other tropical fish: 64–74°F (17.7–23.3°C). Here are some other types that prefer cooler water and will get along well. All of them will eat goldfish food in flakes or pellets:

1. **Gold or Calico Fantails**
2. **Shubunkins**
3. **Black Moors**
4. **Orandas**
5. **Ryukins**
6. **Tetras (Head and Tail Light, Glo-Light varieties)**
7. **Plecostomus** — These little guys (Careful! They do get big!) are shy and avoid bright light, but they're working hard for you even when you can't see them. They eat algae and help keep the tank clean. Supplement their diet by feeding algae wafers (sold in the fish store).

EASY TROPICALS: These are hardy types, suitable for beginners. They are attractive to look at and fun to watch. Most are peaceful, although some, like tetras and tiger barbs, can be "fin-nippers," biting the fins on other fish, especially ones with long flowing fins (bettas, for example).

AQUARIUM SALT

Are you wondering why some of these fish do well when salt is added to the aquarium? Aren't they FRESHwater fish? Well, yes, but adding aquarium salt in limited amounts adds electrolytes to the water that help gills work better so fish breathe more easily. Add one tablespoon of aquarium salt for every 5 gallons of water in the aquarium (example: a 10-gallon tank would require 2 tablespoons of aquarium salt). You won't need to add salt again until you change the water in the tank.

Tropical fish flakes and pellets will take care of most of their dietary needs, but they'll also enjoy freeze-dried and frozen foods. Tank temperature should be in the 74–78°F (23.3–25.5°C) range. Remember to select a combination of fish to inhabit all three levels of the tank (top, middle, bottom).

1. **Guppies** — Top dweller
   - Like to have aquarium salt added to water (see box).
   - Best ratio: several females to each male.
   - Do not mix with "fin-nipper" species.

2. **Mollies** — Top dweller
   - Like to have aquarium salt added to water (see box).
   - Easy to breed (see "Breeding" later in this chapter).
   - Best ratio: several females to each male.
   - Will eat some algae and may nibble on live plants.

3. **Danios** — Top dweller (tend to nip!)
   - Schooling fish, happiest in groups of 4 or more.
   - If you have a small tank, danios are a good choice.

4. **Platies** — Top dweller
   - Schooling fish, happiest in groups of 4 or more.
   - Best ratio: several females to each male.

5. **Swordtails** — Top dweller
   - Best ratio: several females to each male.
   - The males fight, so keep only one male per tank.

GOOD COMMUNITY FISH

(Fish that get along with each other)
typical sizes

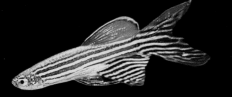

**Long-Finned
Zebra Danio
1″ – 3″**

**Marigold
Lyretail Sword
2″ – 3″**

**Blue
Gourami
2″ – 4″**

**Tiger Barb
1″ – 3″**

**Common
Plecostomus
2″ – 3″**

GOOD COMMUNITY FISH

Bala
Shark
1″ – 4″

Marble
Sailfin Molly
1″ – 2″

Gold
Gourami
2″ – 4″

Sunset Platy
1″ – 2″

Silver Dollar
2″ – 8″

GOOD COMMUNITY FISH

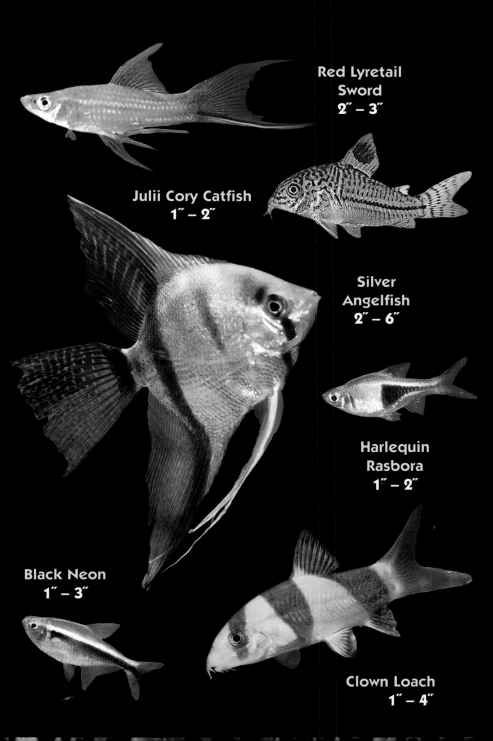

Red Lyretail
Sword
2" – 3"

Julii Cory Catfish
1" – 2"

Silver
Angelfish
2" – 6"

Harlequin
Rasbora
1" – 2"

Black Neon
1" – 3"

Clown Loach
1" – 4"

NON-COMMUNITY FISH

(Fish that sometimes do not get along)

**Red Cap
Oranda
4″ – 5″**
Orandas and
Goldfish get
along better with
each other than
with other species
of fish.

**Guppies
1″ – 3″**
Guppies are small and are
sometimes eaten by other
fish, but get along fine
with each other.

**Male Betta
2″ – 3″**
Male Bettas may fight
when placed together.

**Red Fantail
Goldfish
4″ – 5″**
Goldfish and Orandas
get along better with
each other than with
other species of fish.

6. **Silver Dollars** — Middle of tank
   - Schooling fish, happiest in groups of 5 or more.
   - May eat live plants.
   - Recommended for 30-gallon tanks and larger.

7. **Tetras** — Middle of tank
   - Varieties include Serpae, Head and Tail Light, Black.
   - Schooling fish, happiest in groups of 5 or more.
   - Try Neon Tetras if you have a small tank.
   - Some, like the Serpae Tetras, may nip fins.

8. **Barbs** — Middle of tank
   - Varieties include Gold, Tiger, Albino Tiger, Rosy.
   - Schooling fish, happiest in groups of 5 or more.
   - Tiger Barbs will nip fins. Keeping them in a school (5 or more of them) often reduces this problem.

9. **Rasboras** — Middle of tank
   - Varieties include Brilliant, Scissortail.
   - Schooling fish, happiest in groups of 5 or more.
   - Require lots of swimming room.

10. **Gouramis** — Middle of tank
    - Varieties include Dwarf, Neon, Kissing. (Yes, Kissing Gouramis really do "kiss," but it's not for love—it's how the males confront each other.)
    - Dwarf Gouramis are an excellent choice for the beginner's tank. Other varieties grow quite large and should be kept in 30-gallon tanks or larger.
    - Schooling fish, happiest in groups of 3 or more.
    - May eat live plants.

11. **Otinclus** — Bottom of tank
    - Like to be around peaceful fish.
    - Feed during the day and don't get very big.
    - Eat algae growing in the tank and food that sinks to the bottom. Supplement their diet with algae wafers.

FISH FACTS

12. Corydoras Catfish — Bottom of tank
- Varieties include Bronze, Arched, Leopard, etc.
- Will be happiest in schools of 3 or more.
- Scavenge at the bottom of the tank, but also need to be fed. Use pellets and heavier food that will sink.
- Tend to be nocturnal, hiding during the day.

13. Clown Loach — Bottom of tank
- Keep them in schools of 3 or more when young, but when mature, only keep one adult in the tank.
- Active during the day.
- Scavenge at the bottom of the tank, but also need to be fed. Use pellets and heavier food that will sink.

14. Clown Plecostomus — Bottom of tank
- These algae eaters are often seen with their open mouths stuck to the sides of aquariums.
- The Clown Plecostomus is an easy one to keep; other varieties of Plecostomus can be aggressive.
- You only need one per tank—they grow to be large!
- Scavenge at the bottom of the tank, but also need to be fed. Use pellets and heavier food that will sink.

INTERMEDIATE CHOICES: The following species are commonly found in community tanks, but require a little more effort than mollies, guppies, and the like.

1. Bala Shark — Middle of tank
- Look like miniature ocean sharks but are not related.
- Peaceful, won't usually bother other fish.
- Challenge: Can grow to 1 foot in length, so they need to be kept in a large tank.

2. Angelfish — Middle of tank
- Schooling fish who are happiest in groups of 4–6.
- Best ratio: several females to each male.
- Unlike the rest of the Cichlid family, they're peaceful.
- Like tall plants and decorations in which to hide.
- Challenges: They don't like variations in temperature or water quality. Angelfish can grow up to 6 inches and may eat smaller fish.

3. **Bettas (Fighting fish)** — Top dweller
   - Beautiful fish with long flowing fins, especially males.
   - Carnivorous.
   - Cannot be in tanks with fin-nipping species.
   - Challenge: The males are extremely territorial and will fight other male Bettas to the death. For this reason, a single male betta is often kept in a mini-aquarium.

4. **Dwarf African Frogs** — All over!
   - Fun to watch.
   - Easy to feed (will eat tropical fish flakes).
   - Challenge: They will try to jump out of the tank!

Introducing New Fish

"Fish, meet tank. Fish, meet other fish." Don't laugh, that's really what "introducing" fish to the aquarium is all about. First you give the fish a chance to acclimate (get used to) the temperature of the tank, then you let the fish loose to meet the rest of the tank's inhabitants.

Fish usually travel home from the store in a plastic bag filled with water. No matter how short the journey, remember that it is a stressful experience for the fish. Make the fish store your last stop and head directly home. The fish will not appreciate being left in a hot or cold car while you do other errands! When you get home, follow these steps to make it easier for your fish to thrive in their new home:

1. **Turn off the aquarium light.** Leave it off for at least an hour after introducing the fish to the tank. This makes it less stressful for the fish.

2. **Float the plastic bag in the aquarium, hooking the top of it onto one side of the tank.** Leave it there for at least 20 minutes so that the water temperature in the bag can gradually adjust to the same temperature as the water in the tank. If the fish have been in the bag for more than 30 minutes by the time you get home, open the top of the bag to let in some oxygen.

3. **Gently tip the open end of the bag into the aquarium water until all of the fish have swum out of it.** It is okay for a small amount of the bag's water to go into the tank as well, but the remaining water in the bag should be discarded. This minimizes your chances of bringing contaminants home from the fish store.

4. **You may also want to offer a little extra food** during this process to keep the fish you already have too busy to bother the new ones.

The new fish may be shy and skittish at first, but should quickly adjust to life in your aquarium.

Feeding Your Fish

Most of what you need to know about feeding your tropical fish comes in three categories: What Kind of Food? How Much? How Often?

WHAT KIND OF FOOD? Most of the fish in your tank will be "omnivores," meaning that they eat both meat (fish) and plants. That makes it easy (usually) to find food they like!

Other fish such as piranha—not recommended for the starter tank for obvious reasons—are meat-eaters (carnivores).

Angelfish are among the herbivore category, eating only plants. That becomes an important issue if you later on want to add live plants to your aquarium. There are also fish who prefer to eat mostly insects and they are called, not surprisingly, insectivores.

Like humans and animals, fish need a variety of nutrients to produce energy and ensure good health: carbohydrates, lipids, vitamins, and so on. Fortunately, a well-balanced diet can be achieved primarily through dry fish food in the form of flakes or pellets. Flakes are good for fish that feed in the top or middle ranges of the tank. Use the heavier pellets for bottom-feeding fish, such as catfish. Otherwise not enough of the flakes will reach the bottom to keep them adequately fed. The larger the fish, the larger the food can be.

Fish food, available in both pellet and flake form, should be selected based on the size and type of your fish, as well as where they feed.

In addition to "complete" flakes and pellets that suit the majority of tropical fish, your fish store will also offer vegetable flakes for herbivores (these are a nice change of pace for your omnivores), as well as foods designed specifically for certain types of fish: goldfish, cichlids, etc.

It's good to offer some treats now and then, too, to vary the diet and provide different nutrients. Supplement their diet by occasionally feeding frozen and freeze-dried "live food" such as brine shrimp, krill, tubifex, bloodworms, and other insect larvae.

You'll also see at the fish store supplements like predigested plankton and spirulina which provide a number of healthy benefits such as brighter colors.

When you're ready to be adventurous, many detailed freshwater aquarium guidebooks give tips on live foods (such as earthworms) that you can offer your fish, as well as some types of vegetables and other table foods that can be given safely. Unlike pet dogs, your fish won't clean up the scraps that fall under the dining room table, but they will enjoy an occasional, tiny bit of lettuce, beans, or spinach. Be cautious—learn more about what's safe to give them before you raid the refrigerator.

MAKE A MESS, CLEAN IT UP!
Did you accidentally dump in too much food? If there's a lot of food lying on the floor of the aquarium, use your gravel vacuum to remove it.

HOW MUCH? HOW OFTEN? It is worse to feed your fish TOO MUCH than not enough. This is not because your fish will get fat, but because the uneaten extra food will rot and pollute the tank. Here are a few guidelines to remember:

1. Only feed what the fish can eat in 5 minutes.

2. A fish's stomach is very, very small—about the size as one of its eyes. It doesn't take much food to fill up a fish!

3. Feed two small meals per day instead of a single bigger one. Three tiny feedings per day are even better. If you have nocturnal fish or bottom-feeders, schedule one of the daily feedings in the evening and leave the aquarium light off afterward.

The best approach is to feed the fish at the same times every day and to decide who in your household is going to do the feeding. If everyone throws in a scoop of fish food when they pass by the tank, you are doing more harm than good. As much fun as it is for the kids to feed the fish, make sure that

WATCH YOUR FISH WHEN THEY FEED

Are any of them refusing to eat? There are lots of reasons why a fish won't eat: you're offering the wrong food, the tank is too crowded, water conditions are poor, or the fish may be sick. Pay attention and you'll catch these problems early enough to do something about them.

they are always supervised when they do it. Set up a schedule and stick with it—you will be less likely to miss feedings or to overfeed.

If you're going to be away from home and miss a feeding or two, don't worry about it. The fish will be fine—they will just hunt a little harder for food they missed from the previous feedings and clean up the tank a bit. If you're going to be gone for more than two days, however, you can enlist a friend to take care of the feeding (be careful to show them how much food is just enough) or buy an automatic feeder.

A battery-powered automatic feeder takes care of fish mealtimes while you're away (or even when you're at home). There are also foods that come in slow-release tablet form that can be used to cover for you while you're home or away, for several weeks.

Stress, Disease & Other Problems

You do all their housework and bring them their food, why in the world would your fish be stressed? All they do all day is swim around in the tank, right? But fish DO get stressed when their living conditions are less than ideal. Just like humans, stress causes physiologic changes in fish and, over time, affects their ability to fight off disease.

Here are some warning signs that fish are stressed or may be getting sick:

- changes in eating behavior
- changes in activity level or odd movements
- breathing difficulties
- white spots
- fuzzy or slimy patches
- bruises or tumors
- ragged fins
- changes around the mouth or eyes

COPING WITH STRESS: The good news is that most causes of fish stress can be readily fixed by their human owners. (Later in this chapter we'll talk about the common diseases and what to do about them.)

1. **Poor water conditions**
   Make sure you regularly check—and adjust if necessary—the temperature, pH, ammonia and nitrite levels in the tank. Doing partial water changes every two weeks is also very important. If the water is cloudy in between water changes, there may be bacteria problems.

2. **Equipment failure**
   Is your air filter working properly? How about the air pump? If the water is not moving in the tank, the fish will not get enough oxygen and too much carbon dioxide will build up in the water, making it difficult for the fish to breathe.

3. Exposure to toxins (harmful materials)

Keep chemicals away from the tank—don't use air freshener, furniture polish, insect spray, paint, perfumes, or strong detergents nearby. Cigarette smoking in the same room as the aquarium should be avoided. Never clean anything that goes into the tank using soap or detergent (for example, the fish net or the pail you use for water changes). Also be careful that no one drops coins, toys, or other objects into the tank that don't belong there. You should always have clean hands when you work on the tank, but rinse them thoroughly so that you don't bring any traces of soap into the aquarium environment.

4. Feeding problems

Supplement the basic diet of fish flakes with other types of food appropriate for the species. This will ensure the fish aren't deficient in the necessary vitamins and minerals. Be careful not to feed too much—overfeeding leaves excess food to pollute the tank.

5. Overcrowding

Fish need room to live, breathe, eat and swim. Fish will suffocate if the filtration equipment is not able to handle all the wastes that they are producing—limit the number of fish based on the size of the tank (see "How Many Fish Can I Have?" earlier in this chapter).

6. Scary fish

If you have aggressive fish in your aquarium, the more timid species can wear themselves out trying to keep away from them. Provide plenty of dense plants and other hiding places. If the fish still seem traumatized, you may need to add a tank divider to keep them separated or move the aggressive fish into a different tank altogether.

7. Scary humans

Tapping on the tank to make the fish jump around may entertain some members of the household, but it's a lot like having someone pop out in the dark screaming "BOO!" when you least expect it. Make it a rule: No tapping on the tank and no jumping around next to it.

8. Lighting problems

Leave aquarium lights on for a regular period of several
hours each day. Turning them on and off whenever
someone looks in the tank just stresses the fish.
Inexpensive timers are available to take care of turning
the lights on and off at pre-set times. Monitor the water
temperature when the light is on—if the temperature goes
up noticeably after a few hours, try using a smaller bulb.
If your tank receives too much natural light during the day,
that can also be a problem since it's likely to cause
significant changes in the water temperature. Draw the
curtains or blinds if this is a problem or consider the more
drastic step of moving the tank.

If you have checked all of the above but you still have fish who
don't look or act right, it may be a question of disease rather
than just stress. Again, it's up to you to take action if this is the
case. While we do have "hospital tanks" in the aquarium world
(small tanks set up so that you can keep sick fish separate from
healthy ones), they don't come with doctor fish or nurse fish—
you're in charge of those jobs! We'll talk about how to set up a
basic hospital tank later in this chapter.

COMMON FISH DISEASES: Just like any other type of living
thing, fish can suffer from a wide variety of diseases, ranging
from the very minor to the always fatal. Some illnesses are
contagious; some are not. It's wise to remove sick fish from
your main tank and place them in a smaller hospital tank so
you can limit the disease, if it *is* contagious, from harming
other fish. This also allows the sick fish to rest without being
vulnerable to attack from others.

So how did your fish get sick anyway? There are quite a few types of bacteria, fungus, and other microscopic creatures who live in the aquarium environment. If your fish are healthy with strong immune systems, these are not a problem. But when fish become stressed, their immune systems weaken and these microorganisms can cause illness. Contagious diseases can also be introduced to your tank when you bring new fish home.

Aquarium owners who spend time watching (we should say "enjoying"!) their pets will notice the warning signs for many of these ailments early enough to treat them effectively. What follows is a very basic list of the most common problems—consult the resource books and website at the back of this book to learn more about fish diseases and treatments.

FISH FACTS

1. **Parasitic infections**
   Parasites are microscopic organisms that live by feeding off of other live creatures. In the fish world, the most common parasitic infections are:

   Ich — Ich, short for *Ichythyophthiriasis,* and pronounced "ick," is one of the most common fish diseases. The parasite causes a sprinkling of white dots to appear on the fish's skin. Ich is highly contagious but fairly easy to treat with a remedy from the fish store.

   NOTE: Even if you have only seen ich spots on one or two fish, you MUST treat the entire tank to get rid of it.

There are many readily available remedies for common fish diseases, such as ich and parasites.

Here's why—the ich parasite leaves the host fish and reproduces on the bottom of the aquarium, then is able to swim around and infect other fish. You will need to treat the aquarium for several days to kill all of the parasites.

Velvet — If there are fish who appear to be covered with a fine, velvety dust, another parasite is likely to blame. This is also very contagious, but it can usually be treated with a parasite medication over the course of 10–14 days.

Skin and gill flukes — Do your fish suddenly act like they have fleas, scratching themselves on rocks and decorations in the tank? If they are also gasping for air near the surface and have redness around their gills, gill flukes are the most likely reason. Skin flukes are similar, causing ulcerous lesions. Both kinds are contagious. Medications are available for this. You'll have to treat the whole tank as well as the infected fish.

2. Bacterial infections

Bacteria are single-celled organisms (very, very small in other words) that you can't see until they're causing infections. Most of the diseases in this category require antibiotic treatment.

CALL SOMEONE WHO KNOWS

Not sure how to find an expert who can help you diagnose or treat your fish? Ask for advice from a reputable aquarium store or call your local veterinarian.

Fin rot — Fins can be injured by other fish or by clumsy handling on your part. Most of the time the damaged area will heal fine on its own. However, if the fish is weakened or water conditions are poor, it can easily become infected. Look for a white or gray ragged edge around the injured area as a sign of infection. Antibiotic treatment and attention to water conditions should take care of the problem.

Mouth rot — If you find a fish whose mouth has a fuzzy white edge to it, suspect mouth rot. Treat with antibiotics.

Ulcers and sores — Large bleeding ulcers can be caused by a bacteria known as *Furuncolosis*. You may first notice the ulcers as bumps beneath the skin which later burst and bleed. Antibiotic treatment may help, but fish with large ulcers are not likely to survive and usually need to be destroyed. Other organisms can also cause ulcers and boils. Isolate the infected fish and treat with antibiotics.

3. Fungal infections

Several types of fungus cause disease in fish. One fungal infection causes the fish's skin to appear covered in a slimy white or gray coating. This is highly contagious and must be treated immediately. Contact your fish store for recommendations about which fungicides are most effective.

FISH FACTS

4. Other health problems

"Pop eye" — No, not the comic book guy! The technical name for this ailment is "exophthalmus," and it means that the eyes, one or both, are swollen. Some people believe it's caused by an infection, others swear that it's a problem with water conditions. Check your water quality indicators (temperature, pH, ammonia, nitrite) and adjust them accordingly. Do a partial water change if you haven't done one recently. Sometimes the "pop eyes" get better and sometimes they don't.

MAKING THE MOST OF YOUR MEDICINE

Adding a chemical medication to your aquarium is always a big deal. You can make the medication work better (with fewer unintended side effects) by following these steps BEFORE you medicate: (1) do a 20% partial water change, (2) vacuum the gravel, (3) clean the filters. **Then remove charcoal or carbon filters because they will soak up the medication and this will kill the friendly bacteria you need to process ammonia and nitrites in the tank**. Several days after the treatment is complete and the fish appear healthy, repeat these steps and put the charcoal or carbon materials back in the tank.

Dropsy — Does a fish suddenly look a lot plumper in the middle than it did before? Excess fluid in the abdominal area causes the swelling. This is another case where people disagree on the causes (bacterial infection? old age? bad water quality? poor diet?) but the fish tend to die regardless of the cause. Dropsy is usually not contagious.

Constipation — Blame it on the wrong food or just too much of it, but fish do get constipated. If you have a fish who has a swollen abdomen, does not want to eat, and is either slow to move or rests on the bottom, this might be the cause. Usually the fish will recover on its own, but you can help by adding one teaspoon of magnesium sulfate

(Epsom salts) per two gallons of water in your aquarium. It's also a good idea to do a little research to find out what other types of food you should be offering that species of fish to make sure they're getting a balanced diet.

THE HOSPITAL TANK: Better to be safe than sorry when it comes to separating the sick fish from the apparently healthy ones. Having a second, smaller tank on-hand to be the "hospital tank" is well worth the investment. This can be a 10-gallon tank and doesn't have to be fancy—just a starter system with a heater, light, and filter will do the job. Add gravel and enough plants and stones to provide cover for the "patients." After the fish are returned to their regular tank (follow the instructions earlier in this chapter for introducing them, just as if you were bringing them home for the first time), the hospital tank should be emptied and thoroughly cleaned, including the plants. Replace filter cartridges, too.

Males and Females (Telling Them Apart)

It would be a lot easier if girl fish wore pink and boy fish wore blue—which is just to say that it is not always a straightforward task to tell the male fish from the females. This is also called "sexing" the fish. What to look for varies between species. If you're going to try breeding your fish, you will need to research the particular species to find out the most accurate way to tell the males from the females.

For the species commonly found in the beginner's aquarium, these are the basic guidelines for sexing the fish:

MOLLIES, GUPPIES, PLATIES, SWORDTAILS: These are "livebearers," meaning that they give birth to live young rather than laying eggs. The clue with these species is the anal fin, which is the lower fin just in front of the fish's tail. On females, the fin is shaped like a fan, but on males it is a tube-shaped reproductive organ (called the "gonopodium"). Males tend to be more colorful than females in these species as well.

TETRAS AND BARBS: These egg-layers are more difficult to tell apart. Most of the time, females are larger than males, but males tend to be more colorful and have longer fins. Since they are schooling fish who like to be in groups, the easiest approach is to buy a bunch of them and take it for granted that you have some males and some females. In other words, let the fish figure it out for themselves!

RASBORAS: The female is usually larger than the male, but the male makes up for that by getting the brighter colors.

GOURAMIS: The best clue in telling gouramis apart is that the dorsal fin (on the top of the back) is longer and more pointed on males. The females tend to have shorter, more rounded dorsal fins. In some types of gouramis, there are also color differences between the sexes.

CORYDORAS CATFISH: The differences are pretty subtle and vary by type. In some types of Corydoras catfish, the male are brightly colored. In other types, the male may have longer, more pointed fins. Females tend to be more rounded through the body than males. Again, since they are a schooling fish, buy several and hope that you get some males and some females in the group.

GOLDFISH: When they are mature enough to breed (about 4–8 months old), most male goldfish develop very small white bumps called "tubercles." These are typically seen on the front edge of the pectoral (chest) fin or on the fins that cover the gills. Females don't have tubercles. You can also get some clues by watching the fish—chasers tend to be males, and those being chased are the females.

ANGELFISH: These are also difficult to tell apart, so the usual approach is to buy several very young angelfish and then observe them. As they mature, they will pair off.

BETTAS: At last we have an easy one! The male bettas have long flowing tails and bright colors. The females look washed-out compared to the dramatic males.

5

LOVING CARE
Tank Maintenance and Troubleshooting

A well-maintained tank not only keeps your fish healthy, but enhances the beauty of the aquarium and your enjoyment of it. By now you may be thinking, "Wow, there really is more work involved with this fish tank stuff than I expected!" It's true that doing it right does mean investing some time and energy into taking care of the fish and their living quarters, but you'll find that this process gets easier (and faster) as you get used to doing it. A few minutes a day is all it takes, with a little more time needed for doing partial water changes once or twice a month. Even those will get more efficient with practice.

Best of all, you'll soon see that a clean tank means healthy, lively fish. The aquarium will quickly become a focal point for everyone who comes into the room.

A Few Minutes a Day...

We've already talked about feeding the fish two or three small meals a day. You might want to do one of the feedings during a time when you can spend a few minutes afterward observing the fish. Can you find all of the fish or is someone missing? Do they appear as lively as usual? Are any of them looking stressed or ill?

Feeding time is also a good time to ensure that all the tank equipment is in good working order:

Aquarium Maintenance Checklist

DAILY

- ❏ Feed the fish two or three small meals.
- ❏ Remove any dead fish, excess food, or other "garbage."
- ❏ Check water temperature.
- ❏ Verify that equipment is plugged in and working (filter, air pump, etc.).
- ❏ Turn the light on for at least a few hours.

WEEKLY

- ❏ Use your test kits to check water conditions (pH, ammonia, nitrites, etc.). Make adjustments if needed.

MONTHLY

- ❏ Do a partial water change, replacing 20% of the water in the tank. Every 2 weeks is even better!
- ❏ Use your gravel vacuum to remove waste from the bottom.
- ❏ If algae has built up on the plastic plants, take them out of the tank and rinse them thoroughly.
- ❏ Use an algae scrubber to clean glass inside the tank.
- ❏ Use a wet paper towel to clean the glass outside of the tank, but try to avoid using any glass-cleaning products (if absolutely necessary, spray onto the paper towel to minimize fumes entering the tank).
- ❏ Clean the inside of the aquarium hood. A small scrub brush or toothbrush will help remove mineral stains, but reserve it for this job and don't use it anywhere else in the house.
- ❏ Replace filter cartridge and/or rinse out filter sponge.
- ❏ Replace the air pump filter (if you have one) and check that the tubes and valves are not blocked.

WHENEVER POSSIBLE

Take time to relax and enjoy watching your fish. That's why you have them, right? It makes the maintenance worthwhile!

Are the filter and air pump running as they should be? Take a look at the thermometer to verify that the water temperature is in the proper range.

Turn the aquarium light on for several hours. This may not be necessary if the daytime light in the room is bright enough to keep the fish active.

Changing the Water and Cleaning the Tank

First, we're going to tell you what NOT to do. **You are not going to take out the fish or empty the entire tank.** The beauty of the "partial water change" is that you're going to remove and replace only about 20% of the water in the tank. You won't remove any of the gravel and you only need to take out decorations or artificial plants if they need to be cleaned. The fish stay in the tank the entire time!

1. **Organize your supplies.** You will need your gravel vacuum (for siphoning the water out of the tank and also for cleaning the gravel), two 5-gallon plastic buckets, an algae scrubber or scraper, and water conditioner. These items were included on the checklist back in Chapter 1. It's always better to check that you have everything you need BEFORE you get started. And if you haven't already done so, put big labels on your buckets that these are for

HOW MUCH WATER DO I TAKE OUT?
The math for this job is easy. Divide the number of gallons of water in the tank by 5. For example, 20% of a 30-gallon tank equals 6 gallons. 20% of a 55-gallon tank is 11 gallons.

Since you'll be siphoning the water out into plastic buckets, knowing how much water the buckets hold makes it easy to measure the water you have removed. For medium-sized tanks, 5-gallon buckets make the process easy.

FISH TANK USE ONLY. You don't want anyone putting cleaning solutions or soap into them by mistake—residues from these products can kill your fish.

2. **Unplug all the electrical equipment.**

3. **Use the gravel vacuum to siphon about 20% of the water in the tank into the plastic bucket(s).** Dispose of this water and rinse the buckets thoroughly. While you have the gravel vacuum out, do a thorough cleaning of the gravel at the bottom of the tank. You may want to remove artificial plants and decorations so that you can vacuum more thoroughly.

4. Get out the scrub brushes. Even the best-maintained tanks with active algae-eating fish still need a little extra attention to prevent excess algae build-up. Use an algae scraper to clean the glass on the inside tank and to remove algae from the artificial plants and decorations. One warning—acrylic tanks can be scratched very easily. If yours is acrylic, make sure that your algae scrubber is gentle enough not to scratch it.

MAGICAL MAGNETS

Make algae cleanup easier by upgrading your algae scrubber to one of the newer (and inexpensive) two-piece magnetic cleaners. You rub one along the OUTSIDE of the tank's glass while the other one follows on the inside, removing algae from the glass. Your hands stay dry the whole time!

The truth is that a little algae isn't going to bother the fish, so you don't need to be fanatical in cleaning it. But if you simply can't get the plants and decorations as clean as you like with a little scrubbing, they can be cleaned (in a sink, not the tank!) with a mild solution of bleach and water, but you MUST rinse them very, very thoroughly so no bleach goes back into the tank when you're done.

Unplug the hood if you haven't already so you can clean any algae or mineral stains that have built up on its under side. Set aside a new toothbrush just for this job (again, label it "FOR FISH TANK ONLY" just to make sure it's not used anywhere else).

5. Fill up the bucket(s) with the same amount of tapwater that you removed from the tank. Water should be as close as possible to the temperature of your tank. Add water conditioner (dechlorinator) to neutralize the chlorine and additives. Some people also let the water in the bucket(s) sit overnight, but if you use water conditioner and have a filter in the tank this is not required. Follow the directions on the water conditioner package, of course, to determine the right amount.

MAINTENANCE

6. **Add the new water to the tank gradually, and then plug in the heater.** If you add the new water all at once, the heater can't maintain a stable temperature in the tank. Dramatic temperature changes are stressful for the fish, so be patient and add the water slowly. Starting with water that's close to the same temperature as the tank makes this much easier for the fish.

7. **Replace filter cartridges and filter material.** Most filters these days have replaceable filter cartridges that need to be changed every month. Now that you've stirred up all the gunk in and around the gravel, it's a good time to take out the dirty cartridge and add a fresh new one. Some have filter sponges that need to be rinsed out and returned to the filter—rinse them in aquarium water, not chlorinated tapwater. Write this job on your calendar so you don't forget. The fish will thank you for paying attention to this.

8. **Replace air pump filters if necessary and check that air stones and valves are free of clogs.** Valves and diaphragms need to be replaced periodically—check these if air flow has decreased or the pump is noisier than usual.

9. **Plug the equipment back in and make sure everything is working the way it should be.**

Algae Build-Up

Even the cleanest tank will be home to algae, a primitive type of aquatic plant. There are many varieties of algae, but the most common growth looks like a greenish coating on tank walls, plants and decorations. A little bit here and there is fine, but if the water changes color due to the algae—this is called an "algae bloom"—you have problems you need to address immediately. To get the algae under control:

● **Add "algae-eaters"** if you don't already have them—fish such as otinclus, Corydoras catfish, or plecostomus. Mollies also eat algae.

Several products are available to help clear up and prevent algae blooms. Just drop the fizzy tablets into the tank. As with other treatments of this type, you will need to remove the activated carbon from your filter temporarily so the treatment doesn't kill your friendly bacteria.

- **Reduce the amount of light** in and around the tank to slow down the growth of algae, especially the green kinds. If you're getting brown algae, you may need to do the opposite —leave the aquarium light on for longer periods each day.

- **Reduce the amount of food you're giving.** Excess food in the tank makes it easy for algae to thrive.

- **Get out your test kits** for pH, ammonia and nitrites and take a good look at the water conditions. Nitrates, the end product of the breakdown of ammonia produced by the fish, will promote algae growth. The only way to reduce nitrates is by changing the water. If you have been neglecting the 20% water changes, now's the time to get back on track!

- **Check your filtration system** and upgrade it if necessary. If your tank is especially full of fish, you may need a more powerful filter, or perhaps a second one, to control wastes.

- **Purchase a product** that controls algae blooms.

- **If all else fails,** consider adding an ultraviolet sterilizer to your aquarium set-up. Consult your fish store to see whether a sterilizer would solve the particular problem you're having.

A little algae is not a bad thing—don't take it as an insult to your aquarium-keeping abilities. Keep it from taking over the tank, scrape down the glass so you can see the fish, and consider the rest of it a natural part of the aquatic habitat.

Troubleshooting

Into every life a little rain must fall, so the saying goes. Or into the life of every aquarium owner, some surprises will arise... cloudy water, power outages, and so on. Armed with a little knowledge, some good reference sources (see the back of the book), and a bit of preparation, you'll be ready for anything that happens.

CLOUDY WATER: The water in the tank can become cloudy for different reasons. If you've just set up the tank or moved plants and decorations around, this may be simply the result of dirt in the gravel being "set free" to float around the tank. It will settle—just be patient for a bit.

There are good all-round solutions available for clearing up cloudy water conditions in established aquariums.

However, if the water is greenish in color, you probably have an algae bloom. See the previous section, "Algae Build-up," for some easy solutions to try. Cloudy water may also be a sign that your filter needs some attention—check the cartridge or replace the filter material (charcoal, etc.).

POWER OUTAGES: Your aquarium will survive a power outage of several hours with minimal if any consequences. If the weather is very cold at the time, wrapping heavy blankets around the sides of the tank will help keep the temperature up. Cutting back on feedings until power is restored will help keep wastes from building up dramatically while the filter is unavailable. After power is restored, keep a careful eye on the tank for the next few days and use test kits to monitor ammonia and pH levels.

TANK LEAKS: It's a nightmare—you discover that water is slowly leaking out of a seam in your tank. As long as it's a small leak, you can fix it with silicone aquarium sealer from the local fish store (or a similar silicone product from the hardware store). Unfortunately, you will have to empty the aquarium in order to use it. The tank has to be emptied of everything, the sealant applied and allowed to dry for several hours.

LEARN MORE!
Resource List

There is a great deal to be learned about the fascinating creatures who live in your fish tank—and the more you learn, the more successful you'll be in your efforts at raising them. The Internet makes it easier than ever to find the answers to your questions, inspiration for new aquarium projects, and like-minded people around the world. Enjoy!

Aquarium Books

Atlas of Freshwater Aquarium Fishes,
Dr. Herbert Axelrod, et al, T.F.H.Publications,
9th Edition, 1996.

Aquarium Owner's Manual,
Gina Sandford, DK Publishing, Inc., 2003.

The Complete Aquarium,
Peter W. Scott, DK Publishing, Inc., 1995.

101 Essential Tips: Aquarium Fish,
Dick Mills and Deni Brown, DK Publishing, 1996.

Aquariums for Dummies,
Maddy Hargrove and Mic Hargrove, For Dummies, 1999.

The Simple Guide to Freshwater Aquariums,
David E. Boruchowitz, T.F.H. Publications, 2001.

Hobby Magazines

Freshwater and Marine Aquarium
P.O. Box 487
Sierra Madre, CA 91025
(800) 523-1736
www.famamagazine.com

Tropical Fish Hobbyist
TFH Publications, Inc.
Neptune, NJ 07754
(908) 988-8400
www.tfhmagazine.com

Aquarium Fish Magazine
P.O. Box 6050
Mission Viego, CA 92690-6050
(949) 855-8822
www.aquariumfish.com

Aquarium Societies

Marine Aquarium Societies of North America, Inc.
C/O Larry Burt, Treasurer
4902 Filer
Waterford, MI 48328
www.masna.org

Federation of American Aquarium Societies (FAAS)
4816 E. 64th Street
Indianapolis, IN 46220-4728

Web Sites

www.aquariumhobbyist.com
www.aquariacentral.com
www.fishgeeks.com

Public Aquariums

For a fish lover, public aquaiums are an educational and enter-taining experience, and provide a glimpse of aquatic species in their natural environments. Listed below are some of America's most popular public aquariums. Who knows? You might just become inspired for your next aquarium adventure!

New York Aquarium
Surf Avenue & West 8th Street
Coney Island
Brooklyn, New York 11224
(718) 265-FISH
www.nyaquarium.com

**Long Beach Aquarium
of the Pacific**
100 Aquarium Way
Long Beach, CA 90802
(562) 590-3100
www.aquariumofpacific.org

(John G.) Shedd Aquarium
"The World's Aquarium"
1200 South Lake Shore Drive
Chicago, Illinois 60605
(312) 939-2435
www.sheddaquarium.org

National Aquarium in Baltimore
Pier 3, 501 East Pratt Street
Baltimore, Maryland 21202
(410) 576-3800
www.aqua.org

Monterey Bay Aquarium
886 Cannery Row
Monterey, California 93940
(831) 648-4888
www.mbayaq.org

**Audubon Aquarium
of the Americas**
1 Canal Street
Woldenberg Riverfront Park
New Orleans, Louisiana 70130
(800) 774-7394
www.auduboninstitute.org/aoa

**Tennessee Aquarium
& IMAX Theater**
One Broad Street
Chattanooga, Tennessee 37401
(800) 262-0695
www.tnaqua.org

The Florida Aquarium
701 Channelside Drive
Harbour Island
Tampa, Florida 33602
(813) 273-4000
www.flaquarium.org

Colorado's Ocean Journey
700 Water Street
Qwest Park
Denver, Colorado 80211
(888) 561-4450
www.oceanjourney.org

Oregon Coast Aquarium
2820 SE Ferry Slip Road
Newport, Oregon
(541) 867-3474
www.aquarium.org

Mystic Aquarium
55 Coogan Boulevard
Mystic, Connecticut 06355-1997
(860) 572-5955
www.mysticaquarium.org

Waikiki Aquarium
2777 Kalakaua Avenue
Honolulu, Hawaii 96815
(808) 923-9741
www.waquarium.org